Barcelona

This book is a complete route around the most interesting places in Barcelona, with photographs of the points of main touristic interest, collected in the extensive photographic work of Antonio Campaña.

The route begins in the old quarter of the city, with the Barrio Gotico, and ends at the sea, with its new and modern opening up to the Mediterranean, passing through places as interesting as Catalunya Square and the Ramblas, visiting the works of Antonio Gaudí (the greatest architect of the Modernist style) and the illuminated magic fountain on Montjuic, the Pueblo Español and the Olympic installations as well as taking a quick look at other no less important places such as Tibidabo, Pedralbes and the points of principal interest in the city of Barcelona.

Barcelona
Views

Edicions Antoni Campaña, S.L.
C/ Alcalde de Móstoles, 28, bajos
08025 BARCELONA
Tel: 93 456 43 36 Fax: 93 450 18 89
e-mail: edicampanya@telefonica.net
© Copyright: Edicions Antoni Campaña, S.L.

ISBN: 84-86294-49-6
Depósito legal: 23.105-98
Fotografías: Antoni Campañá
Diseño: Andres Mariani & Diego Lunelli
Preimpresión: JEBA S.L.L.
Impresión: Futurgràfic S.C.C.L.

The city of Barcelona which has existed for more than twenty centuries has gone through various changes throughout its history but it has always been a basic part of the development of Catalonia and at the moment it could be defined as the visible leader of an entire people. From a geographical point of view, its position is unsurpassable, a wide plain beside the sea, bordered on both side by the rivers Besós and Llobregat.

The first human vestiges to be found in this place were on the northern hill of the Llano de Barcelona (Barcelona plain) and correspond to the Neolithic era (XX century B.C. some 4,000 years ago). However the first urban origins of Barcelona pioneered by the first expansion of the Greeks established in Ampurias (VI BC), was the work of the Laietani tribe; installed on heights such as Mons Taber and Montjuic. Starting from here, with some elemental forms of habitation the city was founded and only the orientation of the evolution of urban growth was needed to complete it.

The Romanization of the city took place after the construction of a first walled precinct on Mons Taber, from that time converted into a true acropolis of the Barcelona space. The urbanizing impulse, begun by Rome, took shape in the I century B.C., when, after centuries of Roman presence in Catalonia, Julia Augusta Paterna Faventia Barcino was officially founded. From that moment the columns of the Templo de Augusto (Augusto Temple) have been conserved and the street plan, protected by the walls of the IV century, has been partially conserved. With the fall of Rome (V century), Barcelona became the capital of the Empire of the Visigoth, dominators of Gaul and Spain. In this period we find the origins of the Condado de Barcelona, a title which would be inherited (IX century) by the forgers of the crown of Aragon and Catalonia and which would give Barcelona the nickname of Cuidad Condal. The first expansion of the city was in the XIII century when Jaime I built a new wall. Under his rein the Casa de Barcelona reunited its four crowns.

The expansion of the city was a reflection of the growth of Catalonia. Under the reign of Pedro el Cere-monioso (XIV century), a third wall enlarged Barcelona again; these three constructions characterized exactly the old city before the growth, which from the end of the XIX century would form the new Barcelona, enlarged to new areas by the architect Idelfons Cerdá. The growth which shaped the current city has its roots in these origins and around the age old history of Catalonia.

Various aspects of the old Barcelona, the Roman wall, the Royal Atarazanas (shipyards), the dragon and the umbrella in the Plá de la Boqueria and on the right Puerta de Santa Madrona.

On top of the Roman wall we find a chapel which connects to the Gothic Quarter. The view from Via Laietana shows us the spires and the towers of the Cathedral.

In this first part of the book we are going to visit the oldest part of the city, the Barrio Gotico (Gothic quarter), the Barcelona Acropolis, the civic and monumental

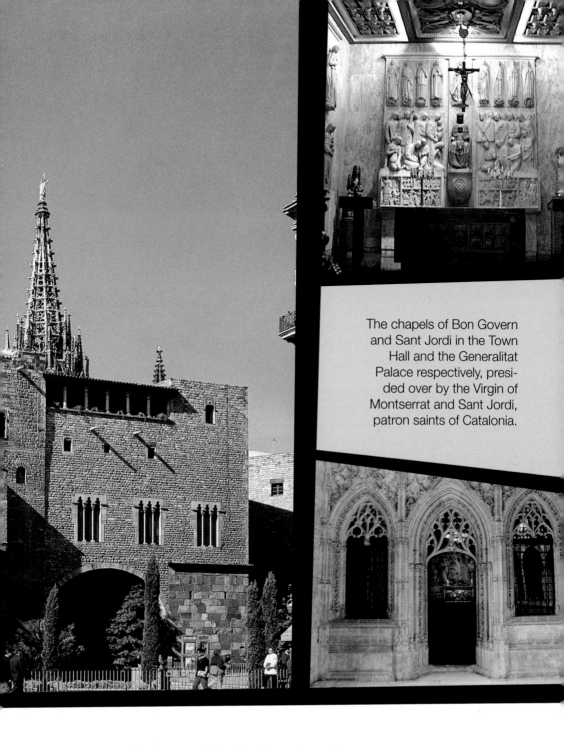

The chapels of Bon Govern
and Sant Jordi in the Town
Hall and the Generalitat
Palace respectively, presi-
ded over by the Virgin of
Montserrat and Sant Jordi,
patron saints of Catalonia.

testimony of the first Barcelonese. This area is
representative of the era of Catalonia's greatest
splendour, when it dominated the Mediterranean.

An impressive view of the façade of the Cathedral from Plaça Nova. The work was begun in the XII Century, on the ruins of the two earlier Cathedrals.

In this area we find the Generalitat Palace and the Town Hall, Plaza del Rei, the Cathedral and the churches of Saint Just and Saint Pastor, the Basilica of the Pi, the church of Santa Maria del Mar, the house of the Cononjes and many other architectural monuments including the Picasso Museum in Montcada Street.

Above left: Barcelo
Cathedral cloisters duri
Easter and the "ou co
balla" (dancing egg). Belc
one of the many geese
Santa Eulária, in the pon
of the Cathedral cloiste
On the right: a spectacu
nocturnal view of Barcelo
Cathedr

The upper photo shows the main façade of the Generalitat Palace from Sant Jaume Square. Below left: the cloister of the Generalitat which leads to the Pati dels Taronjes and the Sant Jordi Chapel. On the right: a detail of the sculpture of Sant Jordi which presides over the façade of the Generalitat Palace.

Various aspects of the Casa de la Ciutat. Above: the Saló de la Regencia and left: an exhibition by Castellers in Plaça Sant Jaume. Below: the Town Hall cloister and right: a view of the Neoclassic façade of the Casa de la Cuitat, where we can see the flags of Catalonia, Spain and Barcelona unfurling in the breeze.

Left: a spectacular photograph of the interior of the Gothic Basilica of Santa Maria del Mar, one of the most representative works of Catalan Gothic, dating from the XII Century. On the right: two aspects of the Picasso Museum in Montcada Street, Barcelona, where there are many noble buildings such as Berenguer d'Aguilar Palace, one of the three palaces which form the Picasso Museum. Below: a stairway in the interior of the same palace.

Now we enter one of the areas of greatest interest for tourists and citizens alike, the area around Plaza Catalunya and the Ramblas, a meeting place for all those who love to stroll around the city. This street which connects Plaza Catalunya to the sea is full of shops, monuments and places to visit, above all the characteristic flower stalls.

An impressive and significant photograph of Plaça Catalunya during the festival of the Mercé, patron saint of the city. We can observe the perfect and sober formation of the "Sardanistas" in complete harmony with the composition of the square, the most representative business centre in Barcelona.

The Ramblas, with its innumerable flower stalls, the inspiration of many books, spreading light and colour. On the left a typical establishment from the end of the XIX century and on the right, the mythical Font de Canaletes, at the beginning of the Ramblas. They say whoever drinks its water will always return to Barcelona.

Walking down from Plaza Catalunya on one side or another of the Ramblas we find, Canaletes Fountain, Betlem Church, the Virreina Palace, the Boqueria Market, the old "Puerta Ferrissa" and the Santa Creu Hospital. Enjoying an animated stroll beneath its shady trees we can observe the activity on the Ramblas at all hours, the artists, mimics and extravagant personalities who wish to show off their abilities.

Going down the Ramblas we find this original mosaic by Miró in the centre. Left: the façade of the Gran Teatre del Liceu Opera House and right: an exuberant flower stall.

Once past the flower stalls, in front of the remodelled Liceu Opera House, at the heart of the Ramblas we can see a central design by Miró. Beautiful buildings of great interest decorated in the Modernist style flank both sides and a few meters further down we find Nou de La Rambla Street and the Güell Palace, one of the great works of Gaudí. Just across the street there is one of the most beautiful squares in the city, Plaza Real. The street lamps here were also designed by Gaudí.

From the same level as Plaza Reial the statue of Colon is now visible and walking toward it we pass the Pompeu Fabra University and the Arc del Teatre, with its monument to Pitarra. From here the Ramblas opens up to the sea, leaving us in Portal de la Pau, where most of the buildings belong to the Navy, among those the royal Draçanes.

One of the more Mediterranean characteristics of Barcelona could be its maritime vocation, demonstrated by the attractions offered in the Portal del Pau, with the monument to Columbus, Marina and Port Vell and Maremagnum, a wide variety in a small space.

The monumental work of Antonio Gaudí is another important part of Barcelona's history. Without doubt he was the most original and popular genius of Modernism, the architectural current which was widely accepted in Barcelona with Gaudí as its star.

The Sagrada Familia with its majestic and impressive spires is without doubt the masterpiece of Antoni Gaudí, the great architect of Modernism in Barcelona.

After visiting the Sagrada Famila, the temple which Gaudi conceived as the new cathedral of Barcelona we can visit two singular buildings which he created in the elegant Paseo de Gracia, Battló House and the "Pedrera". Both are outstandingly original and we have to admire the fact that they were constructed as housing, with such harmony that no detail was forgotten; Gaudí even designed the furniture for both houses.

Above: the windows of the Casa Batlló, work of the architect Antoni Gaudí. Left: the illuminated dome of the house and right: a detail of the balconies, as well as the façade on Paseo de Gracia.

Another of the great
works of Gaudí: Casa
Milá also in Paseo de
Grácia popularly known
as "la Pedrera" because
of its rocky aspect. Left:
the chimneys and an
aerial view. Right: a view
of the balconies of this
unique house.

A visit to Güell Park is enough to demonstrate Gaudí's overwhelming fantasy. It was meant to be a housing estate with family houses separate from the common facilities. A type of garden city in the purest Gaudían style, where disharmony and functional had to coexist.

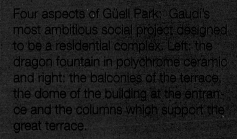

Four aspects of Güell Park: Gaudi's most ambitious social project designed to be a residential complex. Left: the dragon fountain in polychrome ceramic and right: the balconies of the terrace, the dome of the building at the entrance and the columns which support the great terrace.

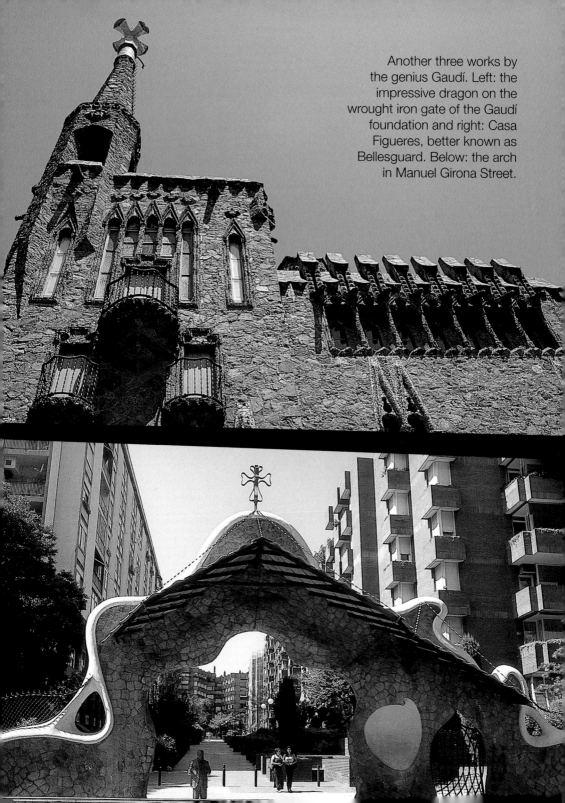

Another three works by the genius Gaudí. Left: the impressive dragon on the wrought iron gate of the Gaudí foundation and right: Casa Figueres, better known as Bellesguard. Below: the arch in Manuel Girona Street.

Other Modernist buildings which appeared in Barcelona at the beginning of the century are, above left: Casa Ametller, by Puig i Cadafalch. Below: Casa Lleó Morera and on the right: Casa Arnus by Enric Sagnier.

Modernism as an architectural current was not exclusive to Gaudí. Domench i Muntaner and Puig i Cadafalch had a no less valued, more balanced view of forms, and their works can be found in the most privileged areas of Barcelona. The buildings in Paseo de Gracia stand out and we must not forget the masterpiece, the Palau de la Música.

Continuing along our architectural route we enter Ciutadella Park, the old army barracks, where nowadays we find the Zoo, the Museum of Modern Art and the seat of the Catalonia Parliament, in front of which we can see the elegant statue "Desconsol" by Limona.

On the left: the calm-
ness of art reflected
in "El Desconsol" by
Llimona in front of the
Catalonian Parliament.
Above right: the
Monumental Cascade
by Josep Fontserre
and Antoni Gaudí in
Ciutadella Park and
below: "L'Arc de Tromf"
by Josep Vila Seca.

Above: the Palau Sant Jordi, by Arata Isozaki, one of the best Olympic installations of '92. Below: the Olympic Stadium, and on the right: the elegant communications tower by the engineer Calatrava.

Montjuic Mountain has always been emblematic for Barcelona. The first settlers, the Laietans lived here and some of the greatest events in Barcelona's history have been celebrated here. The last of these was the 1992 Olympic Games, which gave Barcelona the Palau Sant Jordi, the remodelled Olympic Stadium and innumerable first class sports installations.

The architect, Carlos Buigas, created the Font Magica below the Palau Nacional at the foot of Montjuic Mountain for the 1929 Exhibition. Here we can see three different aspects. Below right: the Font Monumental in Plaza España.

The "Pople Español", another inheritance of the 1929 Expo. Currently it is one of the most important leisure macroprecincts in Barcelona and a visit to it must not be missed.

Great works, testimony to the 1929 Universal Exhibition can still be found on Montjuic. The Magic Fountain, the fantastic creation of Antoni Buigas, is the most impressive illuminated fountain in the world, and the Pueblo Español, a small area where we can see a reproduction of some of the most characteristic buildings and streets from all over Spain. We must also mention the Palacio Nacional, nowadays the Catalonian National Art Museum (MNAC), and other buildings such as Albeniz Palace, the Spanish Royal family's residence in Barcelona.

Above left: Monjuic Castle on the summit of the mountain. Below left: the unique building of the Fundació Miró. On the right: a fountain in the gardens of Albeniz Palace and below the Mercat de les Flores.

Above: and impressive view of Portal de la Pau, where the magnitude of the new Maremagnum leisure complex can be seen. It is an ideal place for recreation with spectacular facilities such as the IMAX cinemas and the modern aquarium, with its wide variety of fish including sharks.

From Montjuic we return to the sea, this time to contemplate Barcelona's latest opening-up to the Mediterranean, Maremagnum, a leisure and commercial centre in the heart of Barcelona's port. Here we find many restaurants, night clubs and bars as well as three IMAX cinemas with giant screens, and a huge modern aquarium with thousands of marine species including sharks.

An impressive general view of the Port from Maremagnum.

Left: interior of the "Palau de la Musica Catalan" Right: "Arts" Hotel and "Mafre" Tower, singular buildings in the new maritime district of Barcelona, Olympic Village and Olympic Port in Poble Nou. Middle: Barcelona Contemporary Art Museum (MACBA); Below: "Caixa Forum" exhibition centre.

The maritime character of Barcelona can be seen in the great expansion represented by the Olympic Port, the restored beaches of the Barceloneta, the modern port installations and the great urban change of the totally remodelled Pople Nou, which was the Olympic village in 1992.

On the left, a beautiful image of Barcelona's beaches
and on the right, as if it were a tiny fishing village on
the coast, the fishing port of Barcelona.

On the summit of Tibidabo Mountain on the Collcerola ridge which surrounds Barcelona we find the popular attractions park as well as the Expiatory Temple, Sagrado Corazon, right; perfectly illuminated in a photograph taken at night.

The high part of Barcelona also has its charms.
From Tibidabo Mountain with its expiatory Temple and
Attractions Park we come down to the residential area
of Pedrables where the Gothic Monastery houses the
celebrated Thyssen-Bornemisza Art Collection. A few
metres further on we find Pedralbes Palace, in the
Diagonal, the great Avenue which divides Barcelona from
East to West, with its luxurious modern banks, hotels and
office buildings.

A mixture of styles and eras in the high part of the city, as are the modern buildings of Editorial Planeta, the Neoclassical Pedralbes Palace and the Gothic Monastry of Pedralbes begun in the XIV century with the art museum which houses the Thyssen-Bornemisza collection.

Marvellous view of the Nou Camp, the Barcelona Football Stadium, with a capacity for 100,000 spectators, one of the best sports installations in Europe, it also has an excellent museum.

Agbar Tower

DIAGONAL BARCELONA